IDEAS IN P

Paranoia

David Bell

Series editor: Ivan Ward

ICON BOOKS UK

TOTEM BOOKS USA

Published in the UK in 2003
by Icon Books Ltd., Grange Road,
Duxford, Cambridge CB2 4QF
E-mail: info@iconbooks.co.uk
www.iconbooks.co.uk

Published in the USA in 2003
by Totem Books
Inquiries to: Icon Books Ltd.,
Grange Road, Duxford
Cambridge CB2 4QF, UK

Sold in the UK, Europe, South Africa
and Asia by Faber and Faber Ltd.,
3 Queen Square, London WC1N 3AU
or their agents

Distributed to the trade in the USA
by National Book Network Inc.,
4720 Boston Way, Lanham,
Maryland 20706

Distributed in the UK, Europe,
South Africa and Asia by
Macmillan Distribution Ltd.,
Houndmills, Basingstoke RG21 6XS

Distributed in Canada by
Penguin Books Canada,
10 Alcorn Avenue, Suite 300,
Toronto, Ontario M4V 3B2

Published in Australia in 2003
by Allen & Unwin Pty. Ltd.,
PO Box 8500, 83 Alexander Street,
Crows Nest, NSW 2065

ISBN 1 84046 377 5

Series editor: Ivan Ward

Typesetting by Hands Fotoset

Printed and bound in the UK by
Cox & Wyman Ltd., Reading

Introduction

The human mind is at every turn of its existence confronted with the experience of anxiety. This anxiety, according to Freud, falls basically into two types. The first derives from the perception of danger in the outside world. The second arises from a site which, though less obvious, is equally real – namely from within, from aspects of the mind which for whatever reason are intolerable to consciousness. These would include drives such as aggression, emotions such as hatred, or intolerable ideas such as awareness of ordinary human vulnerability.

Anxiety that arises from without can be dealt with in the time-honoured way – fight or flight. However, that which arises from within brings a different class of problem. Wherever one goes, it will follow. A further distinction lies in the fact that danger from without tends to be infrequent and episodic, whereas that from within is in a sense ever-present, and so may seem to be inescapable.

However, the human mind discovered an artful way of dealing with this problem. The threatening mental content is transported from its internal position and relocated in the external world. This procedure, termed *projection* as inner mental contents are *projected* outwards into the external world, is essential to the stability of the mind. However, it brings in its wake a whole series of difficulties. For, now objects in the external world appear to the individual to be increasingly menacing, having been endowed with this 'projective significance'. It is this psychological mechanism that underlies all paranoid mental states.

A psychiatrist on an acute admission ward brushed past a male patient. The patient turned to him, his face a mixture of anger and anxiety and exclaimed, 'I am not homosexual.' How is one to understand this event? Following the model outlined here, the explanation would be along the following lines. The man, at a level removed from conscious awareness, might have perceived within himself a homosexual impulse that was pressing forward for awareness. But, for whatever reason, this was intolerable and so could not be admitted into consciousness. He defended himself through projecting the impulse, and the awareness of it, into external figures – in this case, the psychiatrist. Instead of feeling that a disturbing idea was forcing itself upon his own mind, he believed that the idea belonged to an external figure, the psychiatrist, who was trying to force it upon him. Through this procedure, a psychic conflict is transformed into a spatial one.

Projective processes are part of the everyday relation of the mind to the world. They form the basis of the way we endow the world around us with personal significance. Artists and novelists project important aspects of themselves into the scenes they are painting or imagining; this interplay between inner and outer worlds is an essential part of the creative work and, of course, does not usually result in paranoia. The critical difference is that, in this more normal projective process, the person does not seek to rid the mind of unbearable mental contents but instead wishes to remain in contact with them. He uses the external objects as a screen on which he can project aspects of his own mind in order to see them more clearly.

We are all prone at times, especially when we feel unsafe, to attribute to the world around us sinister meaning. Our thinking, we may say, takes on a paranoid colouring. Such occasions are unpleasant reminders of just how fragile, at times, is our grip on reality. A colleague reported the following story.

Before leaving on a trip, she injured her finger and required stitches at the local casualty department. When the doctor was sewing up her finger, she, the patient, asked him questions about the treatment he was providing, something he seemed to regard as inappropriate. She then embarked on a long motorway journey. There was a blizzard, and she eventually found herself alone on a motorway in treacherous conditions with darkness rapidly falling. Her finger began to throb. Alone and vulnerable, she found herself beginning to wonder if the doctor, angry at her questions, had deliberately done something to her finger to make it worse, in a kind of vengeful and sadistic state. As external conditions deteriorated and the pain became very intense, this idea took on the character- istics of a terrifying conviction. She turned off the motorway and drove to the casualty department of the nearest hospital. Her pain was relieved rapidly and, as she was thus once more restored to a safe world, the paranoid ideas receded and were replaced by a normal relation to reality.

My reason for describing this is not to draw attention to an extraordinary occurrence but more to its ordinariness. All of us when under pressures of various sorts, and when removed from the supports of a secure stable environment, are prone to just this kind of paranoid thinking. However, when normal circumstances are resumed, we usually recover our balance relatively easily.

But there are those for whom all relations with others carry a paranoid quality. They are suspicious and very sensitive, easily assuming that others have malevolent intentions towards them. This results in an unhappy and limited life. In those who develop acute paranoid illnesses, suspiciousness and wariness give way to delusional conviction. Such individuals do not feel *suspicion* that others are threatening them in some way but instead become *convinced* that this is so, and this conviction may become elaborated into a sophisticated delusional system.

They claim, for example, that there is a conspiracy by some powerful international organisation which has implanted a computer chip in their brain and through it is sending messages and seeking to control them.

It might be helpful at this juncture to draw attention to the fact that I have been using the term 'paranoia' rather ambiguously. There is a useful distinction to be made here between paranoid anxiety and paranoia. Paranoid anxiety is to some extent universal and, as I will discuss below, has a role to play in a wide variety of psychological disturbances; whereas paranoid ideation, which is more transitory, suggests a more severe disturbance in cognitive and intellectual function. In fact, paranoid ideas to some extent provide a rationalisation for paranoid anxiety. For if I am convinced that various others have malevolent intentions towards me, I have good reason to be anxious and suspicious.

In the above I have moved with apparent ease from ordinary fears and anxieties that are constitutive of being human, to aspects of artistic creativity, to forms of insanity. This captures something of what psychoanalytic thinking is like. For psychoanalysis undermines apparent discontinuities between the normal and the abnormal. The ideas of the insane, apparently so far from normality, can be shown to have in their content much more in common with ordinary human concerns than at first glance might seem to be the case. And certain aspects of ordinary life which at first seem so unremarkable show themselves, when scrutinised more closely, to be derived from motives and ideas which, when apprehended fully, can only strike us as bizarre.

This is a theme that Freud returns to on many occasions throughout his oeuvre. For Freud, a dream, a symptom, a cultural production all have equivalencies in their deep structure that are not obvious. In *Totem and Taboo* (1913), he gives particular emphasis to the relation between neurotic symptoms and ordinary cultural phenomena: 'It might be maintained that a case of hysteria is a caricature of a work of art, that an obsessional neurosis is a caricature of religion and that a paranoiac delusion is a caricature of a philosophical system.'[1] It is the reference to paranoia that is most germane to our theme. Freud does not mean to say that philosophers tend to be paranoid, nor that those who suffer from paranoia make good philosophers. The similarity derives more from the way in which both dwell upon fundamental problems of existence, give great attention to detail and argument, and are driven to the creation of systems of thought through urgent internal concerns.

In what follows I will first trace some aspects of the development of Freud's understanding of paranoia both at the individual and the group level. In the course of this I will focus on Freud's most detailed attempt to understand a delusional system – namely, the Schreber case. Following this I will turn to the contribution made to the understanding of paranoia by the work of Melanie Klein. I will also comment on the relevance of this understanding to the paranoid systems that so insidiously invade our everyday relation to socio-political processes which, though 'normal' (statistically), also exemplify very disturbed patterns of thinking.

First, however, it might be helpful to make a few comments on the derivation of the term 'paranoia'. The term 'paranoia' derives from the Greek and is a compound word meaning 'beside oneself', 'out of one's own mind'. It thus originally referred to any kind of madness. In classical psychiatry of the 19th and early 20th century, paranoia referred to any mental illness in which systematised delusions dominated the picture. The term is also of course part of everyday language and has come to indicate irrational fear of persons or objects in the outside world.

Freud on Paranoia

When Freud uses the term 'paranoia', the sense is twofold. It refers both to a state of mind – irrational fear – *and* to the mechanism through which this state is both acquired and sustained, the mechanism of projection. Given that projective processes always start life as a way of ridding the mind of intolerable contents (as described above), paranoia falls into place as a mental illness originally derived from modes of defence, or as Freud described it a 'Neuro-Psychosis of Defence'.[2] This is again characteristic of the psychoanalytic approach. Many of the psychological problems that beset us start out life, developmentally, as a way of coping with difficulties, and in this sense they were originally adaptive. But when these defences come to dominate all mental functioning, maintaining a rigid structure that now impedes any further development, they appear no longer to be serving any adaptive function. However, this is not quite so. From a psychoanalytic perspective, all symptoms have a dual function: they both express a difficulty while at one and the same time being the attempt to deal with it. For example, a man may have a deeply paranoid attitude to anyone who offers themselves to him as an object of affection. Examined simply, this may seem profoundly non-adaptive. In analysis, however, such an individual may soon reveal how this 'symptom' has a protective function, keeping him away from any situation that might expose him to his own vulnerability, a completely unmanageable situation that in the past has produced a breakdown.

Freud's first writing on paranoia was not published in his lifetime, as it was in the form of correspondence with Wilhelm Fliess, then his confidant. Entitled 'Draft H', it was enclosed with a letter of January 1895. Here he describes a young woman who developed a paranoid state. The content of her preoccupations centred on her feeling that she was being observed and that various sexual thoughts were being attributed to her. People around her, she believed, reproached her for being 'bad', this badness having a sexual connotation. Prior to her illness, a lodger had attempted to seduce her.

According to Freud, what was intolerable to her was that she had found the seduction scene exciting, and this had resulted in intense feelings of guilt. An internal self-reproach based on awareness of forbidden sexual wishes in herself had, through the mechanism of projection, been transformed: it was no longer *she* who was aware of having sexual wishes, it was others who believed this (wrongly) about her. Self-reproach became 'an imputation coming from outside'. As Freud put it, 'The purpose of paranoia is thus to fend off an idea that is incompatible with the ego, by projecting its substance into the external world.'[3]

(What is being proposed here is both a 'general theory' of paranoia, namely that paranoia derives from the projection of certain intolerable 'ideas', and a specific theory that refers to the content of those ideas. For Freud, at this juncture in his thinking, the ideas that were intolerable were inevitably sexual. Though Freud later gave prominence to our terror of our own violent impulses, conflicts around sexual impulses and ideas remained central to his theory.)

So here we have one of the earliest statements concerning paranoia. Although in the development of psychoanalysis, both by Freud and his successors, the understanding of paranoia has been substantially enriched, the above statement still stands. In Freud's first published account of paranoia (1896), this theory is largely unaltered.[4] He draws, however, an interesting contrast with obsessional neurosis. Both these illnesses have features in common, namely difficulty in managing intolerable ideas that eventuate in self-reproach. For the obsessional, the idea is deleted through the process of repression. Self-reproach becomes self-distrust and so the obsessional person continually checks and re-checks his own actions. In contrast, for the paranoiac the idea remains, but the judgement concerning it is transformed into a reproach coming from others.

The Schreber Case

Freud's most celebrated account of paranoia, the Schreber Case, is central not only to the understanding of paranoia but also to the elaboration of the psychoanalytic approach to psychosis. Dr Schreber was a highly intelligent judge who suffered a severe paranoid psychosis. His autobiographical essay entitled 'Memoirs of My Nervous Illness' (1903) details the genesis of an intricate delusional system. Freud was fascinated by this account and believed that understanding psychosis provided an important access to the deepest areas of the mind.

Schreber developed an acute psychotic disorder marked by severe paranoid anxiety. He believed his body was decomposing, and he suffered various hypochondriacal and persecutory delusions. He recovered enough from this state to live an approximately normal life, while, in a way that is not untypical, continuing to maintain a delusional system. This system centred upon the idea that he was being changed by divine forces into a woman, so that God could have sexual intercourse with him. The result of this celestial union would be the bringing into being of a new race of men who would restore humanity and the world to its former 'state of bliss'.

Towards the end of the first section, Freud describes the psychoanalytic approach to delusions. He states:

The interest felt by the practical psychiatrist in such delusion formations as these is, as a rule, exhausted when once he has ascertained the character of the products of the delusion and formed an estimate of their influence on the patient's general behaviour: in his case marvelling is not the beginning of understanding. The psycho-analyst, in the light of his knowledge of the psychoneuroses approaches the subject with a suspicion that even thought structures so extraordinary as these and so remote from common modes of thinking are nevertheless derived from the most general and comprehensible impulses of the human mind; and he would be glad to discover the motives of such a transformation as well as the manner in which it is accomplished. With this aim in view, he will wish to go more deeply into the delusion and into the history of its development.[5]

The progression from a severe anxiety state to the development of a delusional system is a frequent occurrence, familiar to many psychiatrists. It is not unusual for a patient, suffering from a psychotic breakdown, to present himself for psychiatric attention in an acutely anxious state. The patient is aware of something catastrophic happening to him, but he cannot describe it. He may be confused, say that he is falling to pieces, that the world has been altered in some indescribable way. Out of this chaos a delusional system crystallises, which provides an explanation for what has happened. Characteristically, such delusions take the form of messianic ideas (as in Schreber) or paranoid delusions. (As will later be discussed, omnipotence and paranoia are in fact closely related.[6]) One patient for example developed the delusion that the CIA had implanted a silicon chip in his brain and were trying to control him for some malign

17

purpose. It may seem that living in the grip of such thoughts would be unbearable, but psychiatrists and psychoanalysts have found that once the full delusional system has developed, the patient, typically, becomes much calmer, as he is no longer confused. Now, he 'knows' what is happening to him. For Schreber, the changes inside him were all part of what he called 'the order of things'; that is, it conformed to a grand metaphysical scheme.

Freud makes the point, and this remains relevant, that the delusion is *not* the illness per se but represents the *attempt to recover*. The central catastrophe is the loss and fragmentation of meaningful contact with the world. The delusional system represents an attempt to rebuild a world of meaning. It both gives expression to the inner catastrophe and is the attempt, with whatever limited resources, to recover from it.

Freud finds a poetic description of this process of catastrophe (the destruction of the inner world) and omnipotent reconstruction in Goethe's *Faust* (1832):

[Woe! Woe!]
Thou hast it destroyed. The beautiful world,
With powerful fist,
In ruins t' is hurled
By the blow of a demigod shattered ...

Mightier
For the children of men,
More splendid
Build it again
In thine own bosom build it anew.
(Part 1, Scene 4)

Freud writes that, 'The delusional formation, which we take to be the pathological product, is in reality ... a process of reconstruction.'[7] From this perspective, the patients cannot be 'cured of their delusions' without any understanding of the condition that necessitates their construction.

Marx makes a similar point in his discussion of religion, which he sees as a kind of group delusion. He believed, however, that these religious delusions served important purposes, given the condition in which men find themselves.

He did not think they should be 'called upon' to give up their illusion. As he put it, 'to call on [men] to give up their illusion about their condition is to *call on them to give up a condition that requires illusions*'.[8]

A further feature is worthy of note here. The patient's awareness that his inner world is in danger of total collapse is projected outwards. Thus the patient does not say 'my inner world is falling to pieces' but instead that 'the world is coming to an end'.

Schreber in fact recovered much of his intellectual and social functioning, while still maintaining his delusional beliefs. This was the basis of his appeal to be allowed to leave the asylum. Although he had ideas that he well understood others would regard as mad, this did not prevent him from having involvement in the everyday affairs of men and from conducting himself in an appropriate manner. His diary represented part of his attempt to prove that his intellectual functions were entirely normal. In fact, his psychiatrist was fond of inviting him to his home as he was such a good conversationalist! He won his case. There are probably many such individuals who maintain 'encapsulated' delusional systems, which provide them with a certain equilibrium without interfering too much with their ordinary life.[9]

I have not yet made any mention of the immediate precipitant of Schreber's breakdown. According to his own account, his illness was heralded by a very particular thought. We are told that he awoke one morning to find himself thinking 'it must be very nice to be a woman submitting to the act of copulation'. There had been a breaking-through into full consciousness of an idea that, as it turned out, was completely unmanageable to his ego. In a previous illness, Schreber had formed a very close attachment to his doctor, Flechsig, and this was of a very affectionate nature. Unconsciously, Freud suggested, Flechsig was a father figure, and the affectionate feelings were the external sign of a 'homosexual transference'.

The acute illness that followed involved numerous hypochondriacal delusions (he believed he suffered from plague, that his brain was softening, that he had no stomach or intestines). But, most relevant to our theme, he believed that it was none other than Flechsig who was the cause of all this torment. The idea that had broken through into consciousness, 'I want to be made love to by a man [=Flechsig =Father]', has undergone a transformation, and here Freud teases out two aspects of it. First, the person who is the active agent (in the sense of desiring something) is no longer Schreber but Flechsig. Second, the activity that is taking place between the two people has been transformed from love into hate. And we can add a third transformation: a desire for a future state of affairs has been replaced by the belief in the existence of a current one. To put it at its most terse 'I love him' (and thus desire to unite with him sexually) has become 'he is interfering hatefully with me'.[10]

The subsequent development of the delusional system brings a further transformation. Now, being interfered with in a sexual way by God (here regarded as the supreme father figure), far from being a persecuting and hated occurrence, has become part of the 'order of things'. God (the father) is changing him into a woman, preparing him for a celestial copulation.

Freud drew attention here to the close connection between paranoia and megalomania. As he put it, 'a sexual delusion of persecution is transformed a religious delusion of grandeur.'[11]

Schreber's delusional system bears some resemblance to the crazy thinking so well captured by Stanley Kubrick's film *Dr Strangelove* (1964). One of the characters in the film, the mad general, is attempting to bring about an apocalyptic scenario in order to rid the world of a terrible communist plot that he has endowed with omnipotent power, and which seeks to drain away his 'precious bodily juices'. Unfortunately, such thinking is not confined only to science-fiction films, as there are those, occupying high positions in world politics, who believe in an 'Armageddon' that will bring peace everlasting (presumably conceived as returning to a state of primary bliss) and who seem pleased to be involved in contributing to this occurrence.

Towards the end of this extraordinary account, Freud offers a kind of grammar of paranoid delusions. Freud suggests that the familiar forms of paranoia can all be represented as a contradiction of a single proposition: 'I (a man) love him (a man).' The *verb* may be transformed so that 'I love him' becomes 'I hate him', but as 'the mechanism of symptom formation in paranoia requires that *internal* perceptions, feelings, should be replaced by *external* perceptions',[12] this is further transformed into 'he hates me', or 'he persecutes me'. This transformation also has an added advantage, for it provides a rationalisation. If he persecutes me, I am now *justified* in hating him.

Negation of the *object* leads to the transformation 'I do not love him, I love her' which again through projection becomes '*she* loves me', and this is the basis of erotomania (that is, the delusional belief that a particular person is in love with one).

And finally, negation of the *subject* results in the transformation 'it is not I who loves him, it is *she* who loves him', and this is the basis for delusional jealousy.

Freud's understanding of the mechanism of paranoia has stood the test of time. Paranoia would still be understood by most psychoanalysts as deriving from defensive projective systems. Freud, however, regarded fear of homosexuality as central to paranoia; although this may be so in some cases, in contemporary psychoanalysis this is given much less centrality.

Paranoid thinking has an important element which, although implicit in what has been said above, now needs to be brought more into the foreground. I am referring here to the illusory clarity it brings. In Schreber's world, there was a clear division made between the good and bad forces. In his metaphysical system, good forces that were seeking to protect and promote the messianic mission were in constant struggle with evil forces that sought to destroy the project and bring ruin to the world. In this way, Schreber projected onto the external world, onto his grand metaphysical scheme, his own internal struggles between love and hate.

In such systems of 'thinking', there are only two possible locations – on the side of the good or the bad. This is well captured by the recent statement of George Bush in the context of the preparations for the 'war against terrorism'. He stated: 'Every nation has to make a choice. Either you are with us or against us.' The omnipotence of this position is clear. It lures us into an omnipotent world where *everyone* is involved with me; there is no place for indifference to my fate. In this sense, the paranoid person is never alone in the world, and this is of some importance in understanding the genesis of this state of mind.

The evolution of the psychoanalytic understanding of paranoia has demonstrated that it derives from very primitive modes of thought, and that the term covers distinctly different forms. The theoretical underpinning of these developments is to be found in the work of Melanie Klein.

The Contribution of Melanie Klein

If Freud found the child in the adult, and showed how the sexual life of the child lays the basis for the adult he is to become, then Melanie Klein found the infant in the child.

Klein, a pioneer of child analysis, developed an understanding of primitive mental states that has become fundamental to the understanding of disturbed states of mind.

The young child divides his world between 'good' and 'bad' in a way that is both extreme and necessary for development. For a small child, the world is essentially constituted by his relation, in analytic terminology, to his primary object. On the one hand, there is a figure who provides him with the essentials of life (namely, food, love and understanding), with whom he forms a highly idealised relationship; he loves and feels loved. On the other hand, there is the situation that the child is faced with when his needs are not met, which is of course an inevitable occurrence. He conceives of himself *not* as having to endure an absence, a rather sophisticated concept for his immature mind, but instead of there being a malign *presence* that is felt to be the source of his pain and distress. Given that it is his mother who is central to his world, the malign object, though felt to be distinct from the good mother, also has her form. Feelings for the 'primary object' tend to be directed towards the world in general, which is thus felt to be divided along similar lines. So there develops in all relations to the world a fundamental division: good and bad.

This splitting of the relation to the world, although a source of problems and difficulties, is, according to Klein's account, essential for development. It provides the basis for discrimination and also provides a way of protecting the loved idealised figures from the child's own destructive feelings. An important feature of this world, to which I will return, is its lack of ambivalence. Only what is bad is hated, and what is hated is bad; whereas what is good is perfect and loved. Along with the idealised image of the object, there is an idealisation of the self.

Klein described this phase as the 'paranoid-schizoid position'. Paranoid because the world is so coloured by projective mechanisms, and schizoid because it is dominated by splitting processes. Klein's account emphasises the constant interplay between inner and outer world through the processes of projection and introjection, which constitute our most basic relation to the world around us. The child full of hating feelings projects these feelings into the important figures in his life. However, these figures are then introjected (that is, taken into the self), resulting in further persecution, which necessitates re-projection and so on. We see the residues of this in everyday experience. When we feel hateful towards the world, our experience of it is coloured by those feelings. The invalid in hospital may come to hate the environment he is in and to experience it as cold and hateful towards him. A patient in analysis may have powerful feelings of hatred towards his analyst, who stirs up feelings of longing and then abandons him. The hatred, however, is projected, and he thus comes to feel that his analyst hates him and, correspondingly, the patient behaves fearfully towards him.

This explanation, through its more detailed understanding of the complex interrelationship between internal and external, provides a richer account of the typical paranoid psychotic world. Such patients conceive of themselves as having a special relation to good and evil forces. This can take place on a grand metaphysical scale or their concerns can be more local.

For example, a psychotic young woman felt she had to protect all the patients from the evil doctors and nurses who, she believed, were determined on sexually abusing all the patients. She had located good aspects of herself in the patients who had to be protected from her own violent sexual impulses, now located in the doctors.

We find the more normal variant of this situation in fairy tales and also in religion. The interminable struggles between good and evil forces, so basic to all religious doctrine, from this point of view derive from our projection onto the heavens of the division in our own minds. Fairy tales give representation to powerful internal struggles: the need to protect idealised internal objects from persecutors, and the use of omnipotence (magic etc.) to perform this task.

The pull towards dividing the world in simple ways between good and bad forces, a feature of all of us, usually does not result in illness. However, it can become the basis of serious pathology in individuals and also in groups who become dominated by this form of thinking. Perhaps it is helpful here to distinguish paranoid states, which may be transient and which we are all prey to, from paranoid structures that function as institutions whether in the mind of the individual or part of a larger social formation.

Mrs S. creates within the analytic situation a rosy idealised atmosphere. She makes it clear that she regards her psychotherapist as far superior to the 'stupid unfeeling' psychiatrist who she sees in the outpatient department of a psychiatric hospital. In one session she recounts how as a child, in order to escape from a very persecuting situation at home, she went out to the hills and holed up in a cave. There she 'painted over all the cracks in the walls of the cave with magic paint, to stop the monsters getting in'. Subsequently the therapist made an error as regards the age of one of her children. The atmosphere of the session suddenly changed. She accused the therapist of never having listened to her, of being useless and interested only in his own theories etc.

One might say that, in a way that reflected her childhood concerns, Mrs. S. had used the magic paint of idealisation to transform the therapeutic situation into a protected retreat, all hostile feelings being directed elsewhere, towards the incompetent psychiatrists. But as is the case with all idealisation, the slightest crack, the psychotherapist's error, caused a total collapse, and the monsters, namely her own feelings of frustration and hatred, now had free access.

Some time later, I was confronted with a situation which has certain similarities, in terms of content, to the one just described, but which represents a far more disturbed state of mind.

Ms F. was found by the community team cowering in her flat, having locked all the doors and taped over all the cracks in doors and windows to prevent, as she explained, the entry of evil rays into her flat.

In the above I have described how aspects of the self are projected into objects which then take on those projective characteristics. Klein introduced a new term to describe these processes, 'projective identification'. This describes the unconscious phantasy whereby various aspects of the self are split off and projected, in the ways we have been considering. Given that this is a deep and primitive phantasy, it is inevitably closely linked to bodily experiences. A child, who expresses his hatred through his desire to bite and swallow figures in his life which are felt to menace him, may become terrified of a box or cupboard in his bedroom which he thinks harbours a terrifying monster that threatens to tear him to pieces and swallow him up. (This is one source of night terrors.)

Although Klein is clear that the processes she is describing take place in phantasy, their effects are impressively real. The child, through the projective process, really does lose touch with his own murderous feelings, which are now located elsewhere, in his room, in a cupboard. In this sense he *really has* lost part of himself.

This tendency endures in all of us to some extent. We tend to locate in others unmanageable aspects of ourselves. For example, someone who cannot manage his own more disturbing sexual feelings may tend to see as being sexually rampant and perverse some particular group of people who, for whatever reason, provide a suitable target for this projection. His intolerance towards those feelings becomes intolerance of the others who have come to represent them. Such mechanisms underlie various types of prejudices, most especially racism.

Klein describes the effects on the subject's mental state that are consequent upon the use of these primitive mental mechanisms, and shows how these processes become the basis of some fundamental infantile anxiety situations. She recognised these processes as vividly illustrated in Ravel's opera *L'Enfant et les sortilèges* (*The Child and the Enchantment*, 1925).[13] The child in the opera, after arguing with his mother about not wanting to do his homework, attacks various objects (which includes smashing a tea-pot, trying to stab a squirrel and making a furious assault upon a grandfather clock which involves removing the pendulum). The objects that have been attacked swell up, come to life and persecute him. But, when he shows concern for a squirrel that has been bitten and binds the little creature's paw, the world is restored to order.

Projective Identification as a Means of Control

Klein stressed that an important motive for projective identification lies in the wish to control the object. She refers to a deep unconscious phantasy where parts of the self are felt to enter the other and control him from within. This situation is the basis of some of our most primitive fears, for the person who functions in this way lives in dread of the same procedure being carried out upon himself. The situation, described above, where a patient believed a silicon chip had been implanted in his brain and was controlling him from within, can now be seen as deriving from the type of unconscious phantasy which Melanie Klein had described. The film *Alien* (1979) gives vivid representation to these processes which, no doubt, accounts for its gripping power. The alien monster reproduces by impregnating humans with tiny embryos which grow inside their host and then, literally, tear him apart. Spying on others, a less concrete form of invasion and control, is a related theme which has particular cinematic appeal. In the film *The Conversation* (1974), the central character is a surveillance expert who, however, keeps his own personal details strictly secret. In a scene he plants a 'bug' by a toilet cistern in a hotel room so that he can hear the conversations next door. When he breaks down he hallucinates his own toilet filling up and overflowing into his apartment. This might be thought of as giving representation to the link in the mind between bodily and psychological invasion. Through his omnipotent (anal) entry into the next-door room, which might be imagined as representing invasion of the primal scene, he takes control of it. However, as he breaks down, 'I control them' transforms terrifyingly into 'they control me'. In the final denouement his enemies repeatedly telephone him letting him know that they now have *his* whereabouts, it is *he* who is under surveillance.

Ms F., a very ill patient, lives in dread of being violently invaded and controlled. She lies on the couch in every session in a state of terror. In one session, after allowing the analyst to have more contact with her in a way that felt more benign, she was able to tell him that, as she walked behind him on her way from the waiting room to the consulting room, she felt irresistibly drawn to staring at his anal area in a way she clearly found very invasive and threatening. It became clear that when she lay on the couch these invasive aspects of herself were now felt to be located in the analyst who was experienced as boring into her with his eyes. She thus felt utterly controlled and unable to move.

The close relationship between omnipotent wishes for total control and paranoia is also of more general sociological importance, as Mike Davis has shown in his discussion of the kinds of paranoid anxiety that are characteristic of modern urban life.[14] He suggests that the resort to increasingly extreme forms of security and control does not lead, as one might expect, to greater feelings of safety, but quite the reverse – the level of urban paranoia is ever increasing. It might be rejoined that, given the increased level of threat, this is not paranoia but rational judgement. But, as Davis points out, this situation has little to do with rational processes. The citizens of Pompeii, despite the real threat of Mount Vesuvius in their immediate vicinity, do not live in a chronic paranoid condition. Contrary to what may seem to be the case, it is the wish for control that actually contributes to urban paranoia. The grandiose demand for complete security creates ever more, in our minds, enemies endowed with our own omnipotence who are imagined as seeking to control us. In other words, it is a vicious circle of omnipotence and projection.

A Brief Note on Paranoia and the Superego

Freud described the process whereby the prohibitions and injunctions of parental authority are installed in the mind of the child, as the superego that judges us and whose surface manifestation we experience as conscience. He was struck, however, by the ferocity of the superego and thought this was unlikely to be entirely explicable through actual experience (of parental authority). This archaic quality suggested to him, and here he acknowledges Klein, that its origin must be partly derived from projection into it of primitive feelings that derive from the child himself. This is closely in accord with Klein's model of the vicious circle of projection–introjection described above.

This primitive persecuting superego has received a great deal of attention in the psychoanalytic literature, but for our present purposes I wish only to draw its connection to certain paranoid states.

Mr P., a very inhibited man, was tormented by a terrifying superego. He arrived late for his first session. He was clearly anxious and talked in a hurried way, offering me bits of history, details of his day and so on. His way of talking conveyed no expectation that any understanding offered by the analyst would be helpful; the whole atmosphere was more desperate. He expressed some worry as to whether he would be able to stay for the whole session, and there was an atmosphere of escalating claustrophobic panic.

He then told me the following dream: 'A huge dog was in the kitchen. It was so big I could hardly move around it. In order to keep the dog away I threw him bits of food, to keep it occupied.'

What is so vividly brought via the dream is the way that the internal menacing figure has been projected into the analytic situation. Starting analysis, for him, means that a terrifying dog has, so to speak, moved into the kitchen of his mind. He has projected his archaic superego into his analyst, who has become identified with this terrifying object. He has to give me scraps of material, dreams, history, not with the expectation of understanding but in order to keep me busy and so evade attack.

The suffering attendant on the feeling of persecution by the superego is, from a psycho-analytic perspective, central to the human condition,[15] and this receives considerable support from literary sources. Perhaps pre-eminent among these is the work of Kafka. His novels are truly psychological; the scene of action is the internal world of the mind. In his masterpiece, *The Trial* (1915), he captures most vividly the demand of the superego for total submission to its authority. The central character, K, is accused of a crime whose nature he doesn't know and yet to which he is compelled to answer. The law is represented as an inhuman administrative machine that demands total and unquestioning obedience. Although K hopes for redemption, the reader – and it is this I think which gives the work its great tragic dimension – knows almost from the beginning that his task is hopeless. His attempts to appease the law, that is the super-ego, gradually consume his entire life and, as was inevitable from the beginning, end in despair.

Despair, so central to modern consciousness, has been the source of considerable psycho-analytic investigation. Although some sense of pain and sadness at the transience of life is an inevitable part of the human condition, its transformation into utter hopelessness and a sense of complete meaninglessness (in other words, existential despair) is something quite different. It derives from submission to archaic internal figures that mock any conviction of meaning and purpose.

There is, in addition, a certain perversity to these situations. For, although the type of superego structure I am describing is fuelled by hatred of the self, it can masquerade as an agent of moral order.

Kafka's novella *In the Penal Colony* (1919) captures this process. He describes a civilisation that reveres as a kind of god the moral authority of its legal system which is viewed as the source of civilisation and order. Central to the legal process is the demand that the perpetrator of a crime submits himself to a machine (the 'harrow') which inscribes on his body the crime he has committed. The victim dies in the process, but this is viewed as almost unimportant.

When the authority of the machine comes into serious question, its keeper himself gets into it and submits to its gruelling torture in a manner that conveys near-religious ecstasy.

Some patients who inflict cuts on their own bodies are internally dominated by a kind of suffocating superego of this archaic nature, from which they feel there can be no escape. However, they do not 'know' it is the superego, they just feel suffocated, and imagine the imprisoning object to be their own skin. In other words, the superego is projected onto the surface of the body. This explains why the cutting of the skin is associated with powerful feelings of relief. It is as if the self, identified with the blood leaving the body, is felt now to be free from imprisonment. The situation, however, is made even more difficult when, as described in Kafka's story, the cutting is associated with a kind of erotic excitement that derives from (masochistic) submission to this hateful archaic figure.

The Depressive Position

The paranoid-schizoid system, though offering ways of managing bad objects, offers little in terms of development. The latter depends on the capacity to move away from this simplified, divided world into one which is more integrated, stable and so able to provide real security. But how is this to be managed? The critical factor here is the establishment of a secure relationship with internal 'objects' that are felt to be good and which can thus sustain the self in times of difficulty. The securing of this internal situation brings with it a profound change in the child's way of being in the world, as he becomes able to have a more balanced and realistic outlook. Now he can see that the mother who is felt to be good because she is present and provides for his needs is not in reality distinct from the 'bad' mother who is the source of his frustrations. Just as the splitting of the object, described above, cannot take place without similar splits in the self, so integration of perception of the object is accompanied by an integration of the self.

However, this situation is not without cost. For the depressive position is ushered in by a very acute and poignant mental pain, which is made up of two fundamental components. First, the increase in integration of self and object provides the basis for the awareness of separateness from the object, the recognition that it has, so to speak, a life of its own. Inevitably, this awareness of separateness is experienced as a loss and so is a source of intense pining for the object.

Second, recognition that the good and bad object are one and the same brings intense feelings of anxiety as the good object is now felt to be in danger from the self's violent attacks. Whereas in the paranoid-schizoid world attacks upon objects result in paranoid dread of their retaliation, the depressive world is characterised by concern for the object and feelings of guilt concerning its fate. In this sense, the depressive position brings into being a moral universe.[16]

If all goes reasonably well, there being sufficient internal and external support, the mourning process constituted by these feelings of pining and guilt can be borne. This results in a release of energy channelled towards restoration of the object. For Klein, these reparative impulses are the source of all creative work. This whole process imparts a new strength and vitality to the ego, now deeply reassured in its capacity to know itself and to protect its good objects.

The establishment of the depressive position brings a number of other fundamental changes to mental life. The development of a stable relation with a 'good' internal object, which is characteristic of the working through of the depressive position, provides the possibility of tolerating unwanted aspects of the self, so lessening the need for them to be projected elsewhere. This in turn makes it possible for the world to be seen in terms of its real qualities – that is, not so overwhelmingly distorted by projection.

This capacity to perceive the external object more accurately goes hand-in-hand with the capacity to perceive the internal world, and this provides a basis for the use of imagination creatively.

The above exposition might appear to imply a rather linear developmental model, and this would be misleading. According to this account, there is *from the beginning of life* some rudimentary capacity for integration which, however, is easily overwhelmed by the splitting and projective processes brought into operation by the unmanageable primitive anxieties. As development takes place, bringing an increasing capacity for integration, small quantitative steps transform into a qualitative change. The capacity for bearing depressive pain acquires a resilience.

Klein was describing not only two phases of development but also two fundamentally different ways of 'being in the world', which to some extent persist throughout life. Each developmental challenge involves a reworking of the anxieties of the depressive position, often resulting in a move back into the paranoid-schizoid mode of functioning. Such destabilis-ation, in good circumstances, results in further development, while in other less favourable situations it can bring profound regression and illness. It is for this reason that Klein used the term 'positions' rather than phases 'to empha-sise the fact that the phenomenon she was describing was not simply a passing "stage" or "phase" such as, for example, the oral phase; her term implies a specific configuration of object relations, anxieties and defences which persist throughout life.'[17]

This has important consequences as, under

stress arising from internal or external factors, each of us can easily regress in a defensive way to these more primitive modes of functioning.

Freud's *Weltanschauung* is aptly termed 'tragic', in that pain and suffering are inevitable aspects of the human condition, and Klein's model, with its emphasis on the inescapability of the pain of awareness of vulnerability, dependence and the inevitability of death, is firmly located in this tradition. But it is also true that the feelings of confidence gained from the working over of the anxieties of the depressive position bring the capacity for passion and joy.

Some Further Characteristics of Paranoid Situations

Given that paranoia derives from projection of intolerable aspects of the self, it can readily be seen that the character of the paranoia will necessarily derive from what it is that has been projected.

Our attitude to that which we have projected varies considerably. One might imagine that an individual would seek to put as much distance as possible between themselves and the objects of projection. Thus, if an individual projects his own hated vulnerability into a particular social group such as blacks, asylum seekers or whoever, it would appear to be in his interests to keep away from them. But this is very often not the case, for reasons that will become apparent.

There is a well-known Jewish story concerning a man who is the only survivor of a shipwreck. He is washed up onto a desert island where, miraculously, he survives for a number of years. Eventually a boat appears on the horizon, and frantically he signals. Rescuers come to collect him, but before he will leave his island he proudly shows them his achievements.

'There,' he says, indicating a small orchard, 'look, I have found seeds and planted an orchard of fruit. And here,' he says, 'look, I have built a house out of sand, mud and wood.'

The rescuers are duly impressed.

'And look here – I have built a synagogue,' he says, indicating a small building, '… and there, look, I have built another synagogue.'

The rescuers are understandably perplexed.

'Why, Mr Cohen,' they say, 'do you need two synagogues – there is only you here?'

Mr Cohen looks surprised and says, pointing with derision at the further synagogue, 'That's the one I don't go to!'

Those familiar with Jewish culture will be conversant with the contempt in which members of one tradition hold those of another. But this story distils an important piece of wisdom that is relevant to my theme.

Mr Cohen needs his bad object with him in order to have it available for projection. In this way he maintains the system of idealising his own 'synagogue' while despising the other.

The hater of blacks, Jews or homosexuals is inordinately preoccupied with them; he needs to keep them in mind as they are holders of all those aspects of himself which he cannot tolerate – be it vulnerability, greed or aspects of their sexual life.

A patient in a group seemed always to be preoccupied with her envious flatmates. From what we could gather, they really did seem envious, and yet members of the group had a suspicion that maybe she tended to find people who had a particular difficulty in this area and who she could then provoke.

Over a long period, she and the group were preoccupied (among other things) with her impending change of flat, which was causing her considerable anxiety. The week of the move duly arrived, and the group greeted her expectantly. She announced that she had moved and went on to describe her new flatmates. As her account developed, she began to focus on one of her new flatmates who, it was clear, was envious of her.

'So,' said one of the group members somewhat laconically, 'you haven't moved.'

Paranoia as a Defence Against Awareness of Vulnerability

As already outlined, paranoia and omnipotence are closely related. The paranoid person, as a result of the processes of projection, tends to believe that others are inordinately preoccupied with him, and this, though understandably persecuting, lends the situation a certain grandiosity.

There is, for all of us, something extraordinarily difficult in recognising the existence of a world around us that is entirely indifferent to our fate and thus paranoid states offer a kind of compensation. If you are paranoid, you are never alone.

Intolerance of the indifference of the material world to our fate underlies our wish to believe in powerful gods and devils who are determining our fate. Similarly, the cosmos that makes us feel so small and insignificant is endowed, for example through astrology, with a deep connection to our personal lives.

This theme also bears on our attitude to illness. The language of disease is suffused with metaphors that impart intention to an 'invading' alien organism. It 'tries to destroy us'; we mobilise 'defences' against it. This war-like vocabulary, though in a certain sense alarming, also provides a deep comfort.[18] Some time ago, at the beginning of the HIV epidemic, an AIDS worker described this difficulty somewhat along the following lines: 'It seems very hard for people to understand that the AIDS virus is just that – a virus, doing what viruses do. It has no *intention* of harming anyone. It is really just an unfortunate fact that in replicating itself inside human beings it happens to kill them.'

Vulnerability and dependence, inevitable parts

of the human condition, are however difficult to tolerate. When this lack of toleration is extreme, there results a character structure established on the basis of denial of these aspects of self, and this is the source of severe difficulty. Here the personality is structured on the false, sometimes near-delusional, belief in self-sufficiency, resulting in both considerable grandiosity and a deep paranoid dread of the collapse of the defensive structure. In some cases, the hated vulnerability is projected into others, who become the source of contempt. However, it is also a feature of such personalities that the greatest contempt is reserved for themselves.

Mrs J. came from a very disturbed background that provided little support for the acceptance and working through of such ordinary vulnerability. She was the youngest of four children of an elderly mother. Her early life was very troubled, and she cried apparently 'almost endlessly'. However, at the age of three she 'suddenly stopped crying', and it was as if she had been 'grown up ever since'. The outer character structure, a kind of character armour that suggested a self-possessed young woman, was not based on real internal security but derived from the projection of ordinary dependence into those around her.

From an early age she seemed to have been involved in a kind of campaign to prove that she was always the one 'on top'. Any overt display of emotion was felt to be a terrible loss of control. This way of living served her needs for some time yet offered little in terms of genuine fulfilment, and she was never entirely without the threat of anxiety of a catastrophic kind. She would make frequent references to 'wets', referring to vulnerable figures in her life who were the object of contempt. But the most contempt was reserved for herself, whenever she detected such ordinary needs.

In her mid-40s, however, she suffered a number of catastrophic losses, including the end of her marriage, and the defensive structure broke down. She was assailed by the feeling that she might die at any moment, and desperately sought help from various doctors.

Her state of mind was characterised by the intense need for succour from others, complicated by a terrible self-loathing for being in this infantile catastrophic state.

In the initial years of the analysis, in a manner that is understandable, Mrs J. did all she could to use the analysis to re-establish the defensive structure that preceded her breakdown, and of course this was both inevitable and understandable. However, analysis, though supporting her, was also felt to be undermining this endeavour.

As a result, the analysis itself became the scene of a grim paranoid world. From her point of view, I derived considerable secret pleasure from witnessing her 'downfall'. It seemed to her, and this is not an uncommon situation in analysis, that I was aiming not to help her to move onto a more independent life but to maintain her in a helpless state. She thus misunderstood analytic interpretations concerning her fear of separation in a coming break, as my wishing to make her dependent upon me. She always arrived late for sessions and told me that she just could not bear sitting in the waiting room as 'an obedient lapdog'. Her only recourse here was to reverse the situation, that is to make me wait for her.

Early in the analysis she brought the following dream:

She is being pursued by football hooligans and, running down an alley, comes up against a wall. There is now no escape. She looks down and at her heels there is a small whining dog. She picks up the dog, puts it in a plastic bag and 'lobs it over the wall'.

From earlier evidence and the current context, it seemed that the dream captured something of the situation she found herself in. The whining dog seemed to represent a picture of her analyst whining at her ankles, trying to get attention. But this is a projective situation, for at another level it also represents part of herself, her own hated vulnerability, projected into the analyst where it is subject to mockery and violent attack.

There is another aspect of this situation which is characteristic and is closely related to the theme of paranoia. Through projection, the analyst, too, is believed to hold in contempt the patients' vulnerability. A number of patients have told me of a kind of conviction that psychoanalysts choose their profession in order to surround themselves with weak, dependent patients who they can use to bolster their own faltering grandiosity. In such a situation, it is clear that any ordinary need for the analyst would have to be kept very secret.

Mrs J., sometimes, just as she was leaving at the end of a session, would hand me letters that she had written in the middle of the night when she felt alone and afraid. The letters described terrible anxiety states and fear of dying. It seemed to me that this vulnerable aspect of herself could be allowed to make contact with me only as a kind of secret message, slipped under the door.

Hatred and dread of dependence and idealisation of complete self-sufficiency are to some degree present in all of us and impact in important ways on socio-political life. Our attitude to those around us who are in need, and felt to be vulnerable, is inevitably influenced by the fact that such individuals make fitting targets for projection of these aspects of ourselves.

'Reality' as a Source of Paranoia

It is a peculiarity of the paranoid universe, a grim place full of terrifying figures which paralyses all development, that for some it is preferable to something felt to be far worse, reality. All of us have some aspects of reality that cause us particular difficulty, but for some this extends to an unmanageability of reality in general, and so this is replaced by a delusional world.

Mr T., a very disturbed patient in once-weekly psychotherapy, would characteristically start each session as if continuing the previous one. It became clear that Mr T. would continue discussion of issues raised in his sessions, in an imaginative dialogue with his therapist, which carried on in the interval between meetings. Though at one level this may be thought of as a way of maintaining contact with his therapist, this did not appear to be its main significance. For Mr T. seemed to accord to the conversations in his head the same reality as the actual conversations in the sessions. In other words, they served to deny the reality of separation from his therapist. The therapist, though aware of the situation, felt a great pressure to avoid mentioning it. However, after some thought and discussion, he felt more able to broach the subject.

In the following session, the patient started in his habitual way, discoursing, in a slightly grandiose fashion, on the therapist's interpretations of the previous week. Eventually the therapist interrupted, saying to him that he could see that Mr T. had been involved in a detailed discussion with a therapist in his mind and that he had used this to evade the reality that during the week the therapist had been separate from him, living an independent existence in the world.

Mr T. looked a bit disturbed by this comment but then sought to continue in his usual way. However, after the session he went down to the outpatient hall of the psychiatric hospital and bought a drink from a vending machine. He then declared that the drink had been poisoned.

This was understood along the following lines: what might have been to a less disturbed person an unwelcome awareness of a certain reality, for this patient felt like a poisonous assault on his delusional world, temporarily dislodging him from it. This situation was dealt with by a further paranoid delusion: the drink was poisoned. One is reminded here of Freud's observation that 'the delusion is found applied like a patch over the place where originally a rent had appeared in the ego's relation to the external world'.[19]

This is also a case of shooting the messenger, awareness of reality, where the message, the reality of dependence, cannot be borne.

Paranoid thinking has a certain self-generating quality. The system that it creates has to be constantly kept going, for awareness of its vulnerability hovers around the distant recesses of the mind. As collapse of the paranoid system brings with it a discovery that all that has been hated is not external but internal to the self, and also the shocking realisation that the world-view that dominates thinking is based on distortion, with all wastage of life that such recognition brings, it must be resisted at all costs. Racist ideologies, whether in the mind of individuals or groups, provide a good example of such processes.

Adorno addresses this issue in his essay 'Freudian Theory and the Pattern of Fascist Propaganda'. He points out that the fascist and his followers do not really believe in their heart of hearts that the Jew is evil. He goes on to say:

It is probably the suspicion of this fictitiousness of their own group psychology that makes fascist crowds so merciless and unapproachable. If they would stop to reason for a second, the whole performance would fall to pieces and they would be left in panic.[20]

Thoughtfulness is the enemy of all paranoid systems, as it threatens their existence. This is aptly captured in recent times in the speeches of ideological leaders of the West, post-September 11th. What is revealed is a primitive world-view characterised by a neat division between the just and the good (Us) and the evil terrorist nations which have no conception of morality or justice (Them).

Depressive Pain as a Source of Paranoia

A patient said, 'I know what my Room 101 is.' He was referring to Orwell's novel *Nineteen Eighty-Four* (1949). The State described in the novel has access to all citizens' deepest fears, which are utilised for the purpose of breaking down dissenters. This gruelling procedure takes place in 'Room 101'. For Winston, the novel's hero, it was his dread of rats.

My patient went on: 'I would be in a room from which there was no escape. As I open my eyes in the gloom I can see human figures who are in the states of the most terrible suffering. They look at me not exactly accusing me, yet they and I know that it is I who have caused their pain. Nothing can be done. They are beyond help and I have to witness their terrible deterioration which is without end.'

The situation here is depressive in content but takes the form of a particular type of paranoid dread. Typically it occurs just on the borders of the depressive position and, if it cannot be withstood, results in a return to powerful schizoid defences in order to ward off the pain. For some, the sense of guilt and responsibility reaches such extreme proportions that it results in suicide.

In the novel *The Picture of Dorian Gray* (1890), Oscar Wilde uses a literary form to describe a scenario that, in certain respects, I think, captures this situation. Dorian, the eponymous hero, trades his humanity for omnipotence. He can remain forever young and lead a life marked by a complete lack of concern for the consequences of his actions, in terms of the suffering caused to others. His life is driven only by his own selfish needs, and he becomes entirely guiltless.

Yet up in the attic (a beautiful literary metaphor for an aspect of the mind just on the border of awareness), there is a picture of himself which not only bears the marks of the passage of time – the figure of himself in the picture (which the artist titled 'Narcissus') ages while the real Dorian remains unaltered by the passage of time – but also, through its increasingly grotesque form, depicts the evil that has overtaken him. In the same way that some psychopathic individuals are never rid of a deeply persecuting guilt, Dorian cannot escape awareness of the picture in the attic. He lives out an illusory life while the picture bears witness to the deformation of human character that underlies it.

At the crisis of the story, Dorian has no belief left in any goodness within himself. He climbs the stairs to the attic to confront the portrait, 'his own soul looking out at him from the canvas and calling him to judgement'[21] – in other words, a persecuting awareness of all those whom he has irreparably harmed through his callous psychopathic life. In desperation, he tries to rid himself of awareness of this reality, felt as an unbearable persecution, the sight of his own self aged and ugly beyond belief. He grabs a knife and lunges at the portrait in an attempt to destroy it for ever.

The servants hear the noise and, when they go up to the attic, they pass the portrait, now transformed back to its original youthful beauty; on the floor is a man with a knife in his heart. The body 'was withered, wrinkled and loathsome of visage. It was not until they examined the rings on the fingers that they recognised who it was.'[22]

Dorian appears in a mad frenzy to have

believed he could kill off the guilt-inducing awareness, represented by the picture; but in so doing it was himself that he killed. This brings to mind patients who, in the act of attempting to take their lives, are gripped by the delusion that they can finally be rid of a part of themselves that cannot be borne and, delusionally, believe that following suicide they will enter a new cleansed state finally free of all guilt.

Paranoia's Social and Political Relevance

I have had cause to comment, in the above, on the relevance of psychoanalytic understanding to some socio-political concerns, and I will now take this a little further. First, a caveat. What follows should *not* be misunderstood as reductive in the sense of claiming that socio-political phenomena can be explained *purely* through appeal to individual psychology (in other words, reductionism). Other levels of explanation, such as the historical, economic or sociological, cannot be *reduced* to individual psychology. However, psychoanalysis as a body of knowledge of mental functioning of both individuals and groups makes an important *contribution* to the understanding of such phenomena. The growth of fascism has many causes, but among them is the presence, within human psychology, of an inner pull towards tyrannical states of mind which have utter contempt for human vulnerability. This provides soil for fascist propaganda, a soil which is made fertile by the presence of human misery, deprivation and humiliation.

When projective processes take place at the level of the individual, they can be withdrawn if there is a reasonably balanced perspective on the world. However, it is in the nature of groups that primitive processes, far from being mitigated, tend to escalate. In fact, the phenomena that are so apparent in groups, such as contagion and intensification of affect, bear some resemblance to what happens to an individual when he loses the hard-won functions that civilisation has imposed upon him, in other words, when he regresses. Freud discusses these phenomena in 'Group Psychology and the Analysis of the Ego' (1921). He described how love of group members for each other is always to some extent achieved at the expense of the projection of aggressive impulses elsewhere, namely into the 'out-group'. Escalation of this process leads to a kind of thinking which, if entertained by any individual, would be regarded as evidence of insanity. National groupings are capable of *really* believing they have a god-given superiority to some other group, that they have a messianic mission to save the world. Nationalism is probably never entirely free of such belief systems.

I have referred above to the tendency to project unmanageable aspects of ourselves (such as awareness of dependency, unbound sexuality, violence and greed) into others, and to some extent this is inevitable. Thus (unlike us) another group is seen as greedy, hypersexual, uncivilised. This tendency can receive massive support from propagandistic exhortations of society at large. To suit other interests (for example, to deflect internal discontent), particular groups become fitting 'projective targets'. Racial prejudice, and hatred of the immigrant, are underwritten by such processes.

The near-hysterical reaction to 'asylum seekers' provides an illustrative example. As is typical in such situations, the target group is viewed not as composed of individuals (ordinary human misery might stir feelings of empathy, which would to some extent mitigate the hateful projections) but as a homogenous mass removed from history. The very term 'asylum seeker' suggests a group which can be hated *en masse* because of what they are felt to be *seeking*, and so abstracted from the human horrors from which they are *fleeing*. The 'asylum seeker' who claims to need protection from us is *really* 'on the make', seeing us as 'a soft touch'. If we allow them in, we will be opening our doors to a flood of greedy individuals who will take possession of our common wealth and destroy 'our way of life'.

Entry of the immigrant is experienced, in a certain manner, as the return of the repressed; or, as Jeremy Harding has aptly put it, 'the asylum seeker is now the luminous apparition at the foot of the bed'.[23] Further support for this projective system derives from the fact that, through our colonial history, we are all implicated in the horrors from which so many are fleeing. Through these processes, any guilt that might arise from such awareness is evaded. The more the in-group is whipped up into such hatred, the more difficult it becomes to confront the damage caused, which would bring unmanageable feelings of guilt. In the case of asylum seekers, this appears to reach a kind of climax with the announcement of detention camps and 'fast-track disposal'. What an apt description.

The welfare state gives institutional form to reparative forces. Yet those who depend on this resource, because they embody our own hated vulnerability, easily become the target of deeply ambivalent feelings. Margaret Thatcher's remarkable ability to undermine the Welfare Consensus, a part of civil life that had been virtually beyond question, derived in part from the appeal of her ideological position to primitive forms of thinking characterised by splitting and projection.[24] The right of citizens to have education and housing provided as part of the duties of state was replaced by a kind of propagandistic ideology which suggested that those who sought help were really 'lazy scroungers' demanding endless provision from 'nanny state', instead of getting on their bikes and providing for themselves, as any decent self-respecting individual might. Even those who might objectively have so much to gain from secure welfare provision gave considerable support to this position, presumably as identification with this ideology provided a vehicle through which their own painful reality could be denied.

Where such splitting processes dominate, the capacity for understanding becomes extremely limited. What might start life as simple descriptions of a group of people (e.g. as unemployed, or homeless) become moral categories. How they arrived at this state (of unemployment, homelessness, etc.), an empirical question, ceases to have value as history loses its place. The disadvantaged become in our minds the cause of their own problems, their difficulties evidence of their moral inferiority. The more degraded a group becomes, the more likely they are to be thought of as not quite human and therefore not entitled to ordinary human concern. Thought of in such a manner, they can be treated with impunity without any feeling of guilt.

This process is self-propagating, and its escalation is the source of increasing paranoia, as any recognition of a reality would bring with it the reality of guilt and responsibility, which must be avoided at all costs.

Conclusion

In this book, I have tried to show how the understanding of paranoia, its nature and its effects, makes an important contribution not only to our capacity to help certain ill patients but also to 'human affairs' in general, whether it be at the level of the individual, the group, or larger-scale socio-political processes.

One only has to pause for a moment to recognise just how much the processes I have described in this book are writ large on the world political scene. The righteous assertion of 'our' (human) values over 'their' monstrous schemes take their origin from, and appeal to, the most primitive parts of our minds. Our leaders, in order to serve other less manifest interests, have been remarkably successful in drawing us into such a paranoid vision of the world.

Further Reading

For further reading on the Schreber Case:
Freud's own account, 'Psychoanalytic notes on an autobiographical account of a case of paranoia (dementia paranoides)' (1911, SE 12, pp. 3–82), is to be highly recommended. Schreber's full diary is published as 'Memoirs of My Nervous Illness' (trans. Ida Macalpine and Richard Hunter, Cambridge, MA: Harvard University Press, 1988).

For further reading on the work of Melanie Klein:
An *Introduction to the Work of Melanie Klein* by Hanna Segal is a good source (London: Hogarth, 1973). For a more recent examination of Klein's central concepts, try *Kleinian Theory: A Contemporary Perspective* (ed. C. Bronstein, London: Whurr, 2001). Especially relevant is the chapter 'Projective Identification' (D. Bell).

For an examination of the relevance of psychoanalytic theory to racism:
White Racism : A People's History, by J. Kovel (London: Free Association Press, 1998), especially the introduction by I. Ward.

For further material on culture and psychoanalysis:
Culture and Psychoanalysis: A Kleinian Perspective (ed. D. Bell, London: Duckworth, 1999) is a good collection of papers on literature, social theory and philosophy.

Hanna Segal has written widely on the relation between psychoanalytic theory and aesthetics, literature and politics. Particularly relevant is the following: *Psychoanalysis: Literature and War: Papers 1972–1995* (ed. J. Steiner, London: Routledge, 1997). See especially chapter 13, 'Silence is the real crime', and chapter 14, 'From Hiroshima to the Gulf War and after: socio-political expressions of ambivalence'.

For a discussion of the relevance of the hatred of vulnerability to the attacks on the welfare consensus, see D. Bell, 'Primitive Mind of State' (*Psychoanalytic Psychotherapy*, vol. 10, pp. 45–57).

A recent collection of papers, *Terrorism and War: The Unconscious Dynamics of Politics* (ed. P. Colvington et al., London: Karnac, 2002), examines the relevance of psychoanalytic understanding to the current world situation and is also to be highly recommended.

Notes

In the notes below, 'SE' refers to *The Standard Edition of the Complete Psychological Works of Sigmund Freud* (24 volumes, ed. James Strachey et al., London: Hogarth Press and the Institute of Psychoanalysis, 1953–74).

1. S. Freud, *Totem and Taboo* (1913), SE 13, pp. 1–161 (p. 73).

2. S. Freud, *The Neuro-Psychoses of Defence,* SE 3, pp. 43–61.

3. S. Freud, 'Draft H' (1895), SE 1, pp. 206–13 (p. 209).

4. S. Freud, 'Further Remarks on the Neuro-Psychoses of Defence' (1896), SE 3, pp. 159–174.

5. S. Freud, 'Psychoanalytic notes on an auto-biographical account of a case of paranoia (dementia paranoides)' (1911), SE 12, pp. 3–82 (pp. 17–18), italics mine.

6. The ordinary and technical meaning of 'omnipotence' are quite close – by omnipotence, I mean a state of mind in which the self is viewed in grandiose terms as all powerful.

7. S. Freud, 1911, p. 71.

8. K. Marx, Introduction to *A Contribution to the Critique of Hegel's Philosophy of the Right* (1844). Reprinted in *Karl Marx: Early Writings*, Harmondsworth: Penguin, 1975, pp. 244–57 (p. 244). Italics in original.

9. Classical psychiatrists have described this situation as 'double bookkeeping'. The patient (so to speak) when confronted with the everyday phenomena of life makes two 'psychological entries', one in terms of ordinary common sense and the other in terms of his secret delusional system. Thus one patient described how, on the on hand, he knew that the delay of the 9.30 train from Paddington was just an ordinary delay, like any other, for the usual reasons. Secretly, however, he believed it was also a special message related to his messianic mission. This kind of thinking, in its non-delusional form, is not confined to psychotic patients, and grades into everyday superstition.

10. We now know (see for example Schatzman, M., *Soul Murder: Persecution in the Family*, New York: New American Library, 1973) that Schreber suffered severe torments at the hands of his actual father.

11. S. Freud, 'Psychoanalytic notes on an auto-biographical account of a case of paranoia (dementia paranoides)' (1911), SE 12, pp. 3–82 (p. 63).

12. Ibid., italics mine.

13. M. Klein, 'Infantile Anxiety Situations Reflected in a Work of Art and in the Creative Impulse' (1929), in *The Selected Melanie Klein*, ed. Juliet Mitchell, London: Penguin Books, 1986.

14. See M. Davis, 'The Flames of New York', *New Left Review*, vol. 12, 2001, pp. 34–50.

15. According to Freud, this is the price humanity has paid for civilisation. See S. Freud, *Civilization and Its Discontents* (1930), SE 21, pp. 64–145.

16. All mourning processes are of course character-ised by just these two sets of feelings – intense pining for the lost object and profound, often persecuting, feelings of guilt Klein's account goes some way towards explaining why this is so.

17. H. Segal, *Introduction to the Work of Melanie Klein*, London: Hogarth, 1973, p. ix.

18. See S. Sontag, *Aids and Its Metaphors*, London: The Penguin Press, 1998.

19. S. Freud, 'Neurosis and Psychosis' (1924), SE 19, p. 151.

20. T. Adorno, *The Culture Industry*, London: Routledge, 1991, p. 152.

21. O. Wilde, *The Picture of Dorian Gray* (1890), Penguin Classics series, Harmondsworth: Penguin, 1994, p. 139.

22. Ibid., p. 256.

23. J. Harding, *The Uninvited, Refugees at the Rich Man's Gate*, London: Profile Books and London Review of Books, 2000, p. 51.

24. D. Bell, 'Primitive Mind of State', *Psychoanalytic Psychotherapy*, vol. 10, 1997, pp. 45–57.

Dedication
For Natasha and Ondine

Acknowledgements
I would like to take this opportunity to thank Ivan Ward (series editor) for his very warm support and encouragement throughout this project.

In case of difficulty in obtaining any Icon title through normal channels, books can be purchased through BOOKPOST.

Tel: +44 (0)1624 836000
Fax: +44 (0)1624 837033
e-mail: bookshop@enterprise.net
www.bookpost.co.uk

Please quote 'Ref: Faber' when placing your order.

If you require further assistance, please contact:
info@iconbooks.co.uk